The Ethical Type Indicator

A Personal Assessment Tool
That Reveals How You
Resolve Ethical Dilemmas

Louie V. Larimer

Focused Strategies, Inc.
Colorado Springs, Colorado

HRD Press • Amherst • Massachusetts

Published by: HRD Press, Inc.
                   22 Amherst Road
                   Amherst, MA 01002
                   800-822-2801 (U.S. and Canada)
                   413-253-3488
                   413-253-3490 (fax)
                   http://www.hrdpress.com

ISBN 0-87425-744-1

Production services by Jean Miller
Editorial services by Sally Farnham

Table of Contents

Instructions 1

Descriptive Statements 2

Transferring Your Scores 6

Plotting Your Scores 7

Interpreting Your Scores 8

Egoism 10

Utilitarianism 11

Existentialism 12

Divine Command 13

Deontology 14

Conformism 15

Eclectic 16

Using the Ethical Types 18

Core Ethical Values 24

Reflective Judgment 26

12-Step Process 27

20 Questions 29

*What are the ethical principles
that comprise your personal
ethical belief system?*

*How do you resolve
the ethical and moral
dilemmas that arise
in your life?*

*What ethical principles
do you follow in
your life?*

The Ethical Type Indicator is a self-scoring personal assessment instrument that reveals your primary ethical decision-making preference or ethical type, and the degree to which you are influenced by other ethical principles. It will help you identify and understand the underlying ethical principles you use in confronting and resolving ethical or moral dilemmas. The discovery and cognitive awareness of your primary ethical type or preference can be the beginning of further ethical exploration, personal insight, and evolution toward higher ethical principles, standards, and behavior. This awareness will provide you with an opportunity to engage in further study, self-reflection, and examination of your own ethical values and judgments. It will empower you to better recognize, analyze, and resolve future ethical dilemmas as you encounter them in your personal life and professional career. With this new knowledge, you will have a greater understanding and appreciation of the diverse ethical and moral beliefs of others. This, in turn, will enhance your ability to communicate with and persuade others to adopt your ethical beliefs.

Instructions

The Ethical Type Indicator consists of 42 descriptive statements about various ethical theories and principles. Read each statement carefully, and indicate on the *Ethical Type Indicator Answer Sheet* the extent to which you agree or disagree with each statement. There are six possible responses that offer a range of agreement and disagreement. Take whatever time you need to respond and then select the response that most accurately describes your feelings and/or beliefs. Fill in the number for each statement that reflects your level of agreement or disagreement on the answer sheet.

In selecting your answer, be realistic about your own feelings and beliefs. Answer in terms of how you actually feel, not how you would like to see yourself, or in terms of how you would like others to see you. The instrument depends on your personal honesty and candor in responding to each statement.

There are no right or wrong answers. You will score your own responses and no one else will have access to your responses, unless you share them with others.

Some of the statements may appear to be similar to each other. This repetition is done to gather better information. Your answers to two similar statements provide more reliable results than either answer taken alone.

When you have completed the instrument, follow the directions that appear on page 6.

DESCRIPTIVE STATEMENTS

Read each descriptive statement that follows. For each statement, indicate on the **Ethical Type Indicator Answer Sheet** whether you:

1	2	3	4	5	6
Strongly Disagree	Disagree	Slightly Disagree	Slightly Agree	Agree	Strongly Agree

1. Looking out for my best interest is an appropriate response to an ethical crisis.

2. Ethical dilemmas are best resolved by undertaking the action that promotes the greatest good for the greatest number of people.

3. Being true to my inner self is important to me when making ethical decisions.

4. Ethical dilemmas are best resolved by following the word of God.

5. Written codes of conduct are helpful in resolving ethical dilemmas.

6. If my friends do not approve of a certain course of action, I will refrain from such conduct if it is likely my friends would find out how I behaved.

7. My ethical dilemmas are best resolved by doing that which promotes the greatest good for myself.

8. The decision or action that benefits society at large is ethical, even if it results in harm to some people.

9. I always act in accordance with my true feelings, even when the consequences are harmful to me.

10. Scripture or holy writings should be followed when one is confronted with an ethical crisis.

11. Ethical dilemmas are best resolved by following established rules of conduct.

12. In an ethical dilemma, I will refrain from certain conduct if there is a possibility that others will ridicule or criticize me.

13. Doing what is in one's own self-interest is the best way to resolve an ethical dilemma.

14. When an ethical issue arises, one should satisfy the needs of others before satisfying one's own needs.

15. Ethical dilemmas are best resolved by acting in accordance with the purity of one's own heart.

16. When I am confronted with an ethical crisis, I rely on my religious or spiritual foundation to resolve the dilemma.

17. Following established rules is more important than following what is in my heart.

18. I will not engage in certain behavior if I would be embarrassed if others knew of my conduct.

19. When an ethical problem arises, I seek to satisfy my own needs and desires before trying to satisfy the needs of others.

20. If I am confronted with an ethical dilemma at work, I will do whatever is in the best interest of everyone at work, even if my actions are not in my best interests.

21. A person should do that which he or she genuinely believes is right, regardless of the consequences that may result.

22. Spiritual, religious, and/or holy writings contain the answers to ethical dilemmas.

23. It is important to know and follow the established rules of conduct.

24. When I am confronted with an ethical situation, I am concerned about what others may think of my response.

25. My personal well-being is more important than the general welfare of others.

26. If I am making an ethical decision that affects my family, I will take the action that is in my family's best interest, even if the results are harmful to me.

27. My ethical dilemmas are best resolved by following my inner voice.

28. When confronted with an ethical dilemma, I discover the resolution through prayer or spiritual meditation, or by seeking a divine inspiration.

29. A person should have and follow a written code of ethics.

30. If an ethical decision of mine would not be popular with my friends, I will keep my decision to myself and not reveal it to my friends.

31. When confronted with an ethical problem, I will do whatever is best for me.

32. The general welfare of others is more important than my personal well-being.

33. I make ethical decisions that are reflective of my true inner self.

34. The best way to resolve an ethical dilemma is to do that which is inspired by God or one's deity.

35. During an ethical crisis, I make ethical decisions that are based on clearly defined duties and/or expectations.

36. The thoughts, feelings, and beliefs of my friends are important considerations in my ethical decision-making process.

37. If I am confronted with an ethical dilemma at work, I will do whatever my superiors ask in order to keep my job.

38. The needs of the many outweigh the needs of the few.

39. When I make an ethical decision, it is important for me to be true to myself and not compromise on the issues.

40. When confronted with an ethical decision, one should seek and follow spiritual guidance offered by God or one's deity or spiritual creator.

41. There are certain duties or obligations that I am bound to follow when facing a difficult ethical decision.

42. I rarely make an ethical decision that would result in criticism of me by others.

– END –

*Can you identify, articulate, and
defend the ethical principles that
govern and influence your ethical
and moral decision making?*

TRANSFERRING YOUR SCORES

After you have marked your responses on the Answer Sheet, separate the pages and follow the directions for scoring on the **Ethical Type Indicator Scoring Sheet.** Transfer the Totals for each ethical type to the appropriate box below.

	Ethical Type	**Your Score**
A	Egoism	27
B	Utilitarianism	23
C	Existentialism	26
D	Divine Command	10
E	Deontology	25
F	Conformism	22

PLOTTING YOUR SCORES

Plot your scores for each ethical type. The solid plotted line that appears in the graph represents the mean scores for each ethical type drawn from the representative sample. A comparison of your scores to the mean scores can provide meaningful insight, as is more fully explained on the following pages.

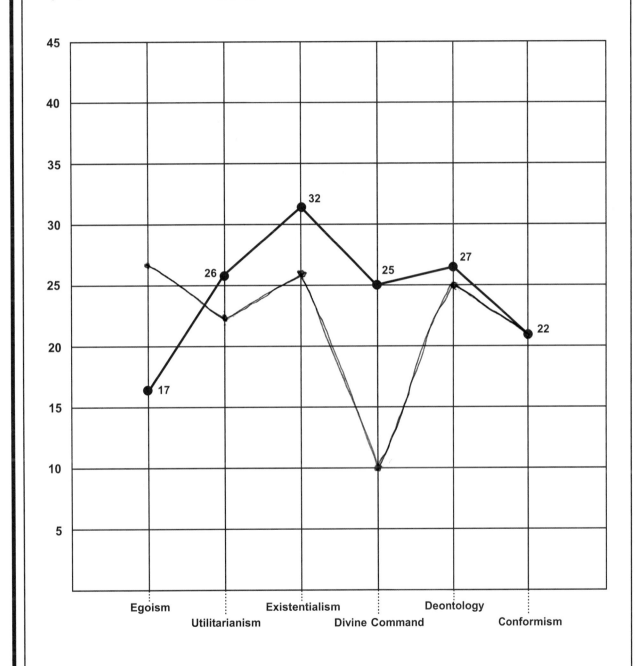

The Ethical Type Indicator measures the extent to which you prefer and use six ethical philosophies. These ethical philosophies are Egoism, Utilitarianism, Existentialism, Divine Command, Deontology, and Conformism. Each ethical philosophy is explained in greater detail beginning on page 10.

Identify the ethical philosophy for which you scored the highest. Your high score for this ethical philosophy suggests that you prefer this particular philosophy and use it when making ethical decisions.

You may find that you scored high in several areas or that your scores are closely clustered together. This suggests that you prefer to rely on several of the ethical philosophies, rather than having a predominant ethical type. This is not unusual since ethical dilemmas frequently involve competing interests and conflicting values that you may find hard to separate. It may also suggest that you take a more eclectic approach to your ethical decision making. See page 16 for a description of this particular ethical type.

Although many disagree, there is no absolute right or wrong ethical type. Each philosophy has been, and is now, embraced by many intelligent and ethical people. The challenge for you is to examine your own preference or preferences and to make a conscious decision as to whether or not your ethical type, as revealed by **The Ethical Type Indicator,** is truly reflective of your internal ethical makeup or inner ethical constitution.

The Ethical Type Indicator also reveals your score for each ethical type. To see how your score for each ethical type relates to the average or mean scores of a representative sample of individuals who have taken **The Ethical Type Indicator,** enter your scores in the far right column.

ETHICAL TYPE	MEAN	LOW	HIGH	YOUR SCORE
Egoism	17	7	33	27
Utilitarianism	26	16	37	23
Existentialism	32	17	41	26
Divine Command	25	7	42	10
Deontology	27	12	36	26
Conformism	22	9	36	22

The solid line on the graph on page 7 depicts the average, or mean, score for each ethical type based on the representative sampling. A comparison of your individual ethical type scores with those taken from the representative sample can provide you with a deeper understanding of your own preferences. For example, the average Egoism score based on the representative sample is 17. If you scored higher than 17, this suggests that your tendency to rely on Egoism is somewhat greater than that of the representative sample.

You are encouraged to examine each of your ethical type scores in relation to the low, average, and high scores of the representative sample. If your score is higher than the representative sample for any particular ethical type, your feelings and beliefs with respect to this ethical type are stronger than the representative sample, and you therefore identify more with this ethical type. In contrast, if your scores are lower than the representative sample, then it is clear that you identify less with this ethical type and it plays a less significant role in your ethical decision making.

Use the following matrix to help you analyze your ethical type. Rank your ethical type scores from highest to lowest, and indicate higher or lower in relation to the representative sample.

	SCORE	ETHICAL TYPE	HIGHER/LOWER
1.	27	EGOISM	↑
2.	26	EXISTENTIALISM	↓
3.	25	DEONTOLOGY	↓
4.	23	UTILITARIANISM	↓
5.	22	CONFORMISM	—
6.	10	DIVINE COMMAND	↓

Are these scores truly reflective of your ethical type?

EGOISM

The Philosophy

Egoism's central and fundamental principle is that one should undertake the action that is in the best interest of the decision maker. When confronted with an ethical or moral dilemma, the Egoist seeks to maximize and promote the greatest good for him- or herself. It is a results-oriented philosophy in which the decision maker analyzes the possible consequences of undertaking certain action and consciously chooses to do that which is in the self-interest of the decision maker, without regard for the consequences to others, how the decision maker may feel about the decision, spiritual or religious implications, any duties imposed upon the decision maker, or how others may feel about the decision maker's conduct or decision. In business, it is sometimes referred to as the "doctrine of enlightened self-interest."

The key to understanding Egoism is to remember that it requires you to focus on yourself, to undertake the action that will result in the greatest positive consequences for you, and to avoid or minimize that which is harmful to your self-interest.

Very few people score high on this ethical type. Of the representative sample, less than 1 percent had Egoism as their primary ethical type. This may reflect that the descriptive statements are inherently unattractive to readers. Therefore, it is important that you compare your Egoism score with the average score of the representative sample in order to determine the effect Egoism has on your ethical decision making. Any score higher than 17 would suggest that Egoism is an influential philosophy in your life.

Advantages

Although Egoism has, for many individuals, an initial negative emotional content, it has been the basis of the free enterprise system. Egoism is reflected in the writings of Adam Smith who believed that each person, pursuing his or her own self-interests, would produce an economy that would result in the fairest and most efficient distribution of goods, services, and wealth. Egoists tend to be survivors, analytical, and acutely aware of the consequences and implications of their decisions.

Disadvantages

Egoism is a self-centered philosophy that does not take into account the needs of others. The decisions of the Egoist often result in harsh consequences for the rest of the world. This can make family, business, and societal relationships very difficult to maintain. Egoism requires one to quantify the actual benefits to self in relation to others. This analysis is often imprecise, is emotionally biased, and sometimes results in unanticipated consequences that are harmful to the decision maker.

UTILITARIANISM

The Philosophy

Utilitarianism is associated with the writings of Jeremy Bentham and John Stuart Mill. Its central and fundamental principle is that one should undertake the action that is in the collective best interest of the greatest number of people. Utilitarianism seeks to maximize the greatest good for the greatest number. It is a results-oriented philosophy, but unlike the Egoist, the Utilitarian philosopher will consciously choose the action or moral position that will benefit many rather than the few or the one. This is done without regard for the eventual consequences to the decision maker, how the decision maker may feel about the decision, spiritual or religious implications, any duties imposed upon the decision maker, or how others may feel about the decision.

The key to understanding Utilitarianism is to remember that it requires you to focus on the needs of others and subordinate your interests to their needs.

Of the representative sample, 5 percent had Utilitarianism as their primary ethical type. To gain an understanding of the extent to which you are influenced by Utilitarianism, compare your score to the average Utilitarian score of 26. A score higher than this suggests that Utilitarianism is an influential philosophy in your ethical decision making.

Advantages

Utilitarianism results in action or conduct that accommodates the needs of as many individuals as possible. This tends to maintain civil harmony in a pluralistic society.

Disadvantages

Like Egoists, Utilitarians may find it hard to quantify the actual benefit to others without emotional bias. Utilitarianism does not accommodate all concerns, and it results in harsh and harmful results and consequences for those whose needs and interests do not coincide with the larger group. Thus, the impact of a Utilitarian decision will fall disproportionately upon a certain group of individuals. Sacrifices will therefore be borne by a small group who may not have the power or sophistication to articulate and make known their needs and concerns.

EXISTENTIALISM

The Philosophy

Existentialism was popularized by the writings of Jean Paul Sartre and Soren Kiekegaard. It is a philosophy that is unconcerned with the consequences or results of a decision or a course of action. The Existentialist believes that one should always act in accordance with the inner voice and internal notions of right and wrong.

The key to understanding Existentialism is to remember that it requires you to act in accordance with the "stainless steel purity of your heart."

Of the representative sample, 53 percent scored Existentialism as their primary ethical preference. The average Existentialist score was 32. A score higher than this suggests that you are primarily influenced by your own sense of right and wrong and you are unwilling to compromise your beliefs, even when they result in harm to self or others, have spiritual implications, impose duties, or disregard how others may feel about your decision.

Advantages

Existentialism stresses human autonomy and the exercise of free will. It encourages internal critical thinking or reflective judgment.

Disadvantages

Finding the inner purity of the heart and soul is sometimes difficult due to human prejudices, emotion, and paradigms. If everyone acted according to his or her own individualized notions of right and wrong, chaos would inevitably result and civil harmony would be difficult to maintain.

DIVINE COMMAND

The Philosophy

Divine Command is an ethical philosophy that is grounded upon spiritual or religious teachings. This philosophy encompasses all religious denominations and has as its central and fundamental belief the principle that ethical or moral dilemmas should be resolved by following the word of God, the spiritual principles of one's personal deity, or a higher spiritual power. Thus, all spiritual-based philosophies are included under this ethical type. Christians, Jews, Taoists, Muslims, Buddhists, Hindus, Mormons, etc., who rely on their own unique religious beliefs in resolving ethical dilemmas are followers of the Divine Command theory of ethics. These individuals act and resolve ethical or moral dilemmas without regard for the results or consequences to self or others, their own internal notions of right and wrong, any duties imposed upon them, or what others may think of them.

The key to understanding Divine Command is to remember that it requires you to follow God's will or the spiritual teachings of one's deity, and subordinate your human desires and temptations to God's will.

Of the representative sample, 23 percent scored Divine Command as their primary ethical type. The average Divine Command Score was 25. A score higher than this would suggest that you are influenced by spiritual beliefs in your ethical decision making.

Advantages

Divine Command provides clear answers to ethical dilemmas for those people who follow this philosophy. Those who believe in Divine Command accept the word of God and act accordingly. They expect others to do the same.

Disadvantages

There is great diversity in beliefs across the religious spectrum, and the word of God is sometimes difficult to interpret or understand. On occasion, it may even be misinterpreted by man. Those who believe in Divine Command are sometimes intolerant of others who do not believe in Divine Command or who have a different interpretation or perception of God's word.

DEONTOLOGY

The Philosophy

Deontology's central and fundamental principle is that ethical and moral dilemmas are best resolved by following certain prescribed duties or obligations that are imposed by virtue of a person's existence as a human being and involvement with a particular profession or business. Deontology requires a person to follow established rules, codes of conduct, and articulated duties when resolving an ethical dilemma. Deontologists do not consider the consequences of fulfilling a duty in relation to self or others, spiritual or religious implications, their own internal notions of right and wrong, or how others may view the decision. When confronted with an ethical dilemma, a person who is influenced by Deontology will search for an applicable or governing duty or obligation, and once identified, act in accordance with the prescriptions of the specific duty. For these individuals, ethical behavior is simply a matter of fulfilling one's specific duties or obligations that exist at the time of the ethical decision.

Many professional organizations, industry groups, and businesses have developed elaborate statements of ethical conduct that are imposed upon members of the profession, association, or business. Some philosophical writers have developed specific duties that they advocate as being core human duties owed to others. These core duties typically include pronouncements such as: Keep promises. Do no harm. Help others. Act reasonably in relation to others. Pay for your mistakes. Take care of your family.

The key to understanding Deontology is to simply remember that you are obligated to see your duty and to do it.

Of the representative sample, 8.5 percent scored Deontology as their primary ethical type. The average score for Deontology is 27. A score higher than this suggests that you are influenced by certain duties that you feel must be followed when confronted with an ethical dilemma.

Advantages

Deontology offers clear answers for many ethical dilemmas and situations. There are generally sanctions imposed for violations of the prescribed duties. This notion of personal accountability helps in achieving and maintaining compliance.

Disadvantages

Deontology does not offer much ethical guidance with respect to newly emerging ethical issues. Sometimes, Deontologists are driven by the rule and lose their own personal perspective of right and wrong.

The Philosophy

In resolving an ethical or moral dilemma, a person whose primary ethical type is Conformism will look to family, friends, colleagues, and/or a relevant social peer group and undertake that action or resolve the dilemma in a manner consistent with the perceived values of the family, friends, colleagues, or peer group. The person who is influenced by Conformism will avoid decisions and actions that conflict with the expectations of the relevant peer group. This ethical theory is based on peer pressure, the human desire to be accepted as a member of a group, and the human tendency to conform to one's relevant societal or family influences. The Conformist is highly concerned about what others think and wants to avoid criticism and ridicule. Concern for the consequences to self and others, spiritual and religious implications, and duties that may be imposed play a minimal role for the Conformist. This person will compromise his or her own inner beliefs and follow the expectations of an influential peer group. Adolescents are particularly vulnerable to this theory.

The key to understanding this theory is to remember that it requires you to act in a manner consistent with the expectations of your family, friends, or other relevant social peer group.

Of the representative sample, 2.6 percent indicated that Conformism was their primary ethical type. The average score was 22. A score higher than this average suggests that you are influenced by what others think and compromise your inner beliefs in order to conform to societal pressures.

Advantages

Conformism keeps you close to societal mores if your relevant peer group is sufficiently broad and representative of society at large. You will always have support for your ethical decisions.

Disadvantages

Conformism interferes with individual reflective judgment. It can result in adverse consequences when the relevant peer group's influence is too strong or misaligned with society at large. Gang activity, mob behavior, and hate groups are extreme examples of what can happen with this ethical type.

The Philosophy

The Eclectic philosophy arose out of the initial testing of **The Ethical Type Indicator.** Of the representative sample, 6.8 percent reported two or more ethical theories with identical high scores. The majority of these responses included Existentialism coupled with one of the following: Divine Command, Utilitarianism, or Deontology. This led to the conclusion that for these individuals, their ethical type was a combination of equally competing influences. Reports from these subjects indicated that they tended to rely on the best of several theories and were not primarily influenced by a single ethical type—hence the formulation of a new ethical type known as "Eclectic."

The Ethical Type Indicator does not specifically measure for this ethical type, but its existence must be recognized and those individuals who scored high on two or more ethical types should consider including themselves in this ethical type.

The key to understanding this philosophy is to remember that it results from the competing influences of several ethical types and is therefore a blend of ethical types uniquely reflective of the decision maker's ethical preferences.

Advantages

Eclectics tend to gather information and deliberate more about an ethical decision. This is natural given the competing influences of several ethical theories. They are reflective in their ethical choices.

Disadvantages

The competing influences of several ethical types may make the decision-making process an agonizing and difficult one for the Eclectic. On occasion, the ethical decision of an Eclectic will appear to be inconsistent with prior decisions or conduct.

Knowing your ethical type
is just the beginning.

The Ethical Type Indicator has three primary applications. First, it can be used as a springboard for further self-exploration of your ethical and moral values. Second, it can be an effective tool for understanding the ethical and moral diversity of others. Third, it can be a powerful communication device for persuading others to understand and accept your ethical and moral positions.

Self-Exploration

The Ethical Type Indicator assesses six ways in which people confront and resolve ethical and moral dilemmas. Your high score is suggestive of the primary and underlying ethical system that you rely on in your decision making. You can use the knowledge of your high score to begin an exciting process of self-exploration and discovery by asking yourself the following questions:

- Is your ethical type truly reflective of the way in which you resolve ethical dilemmas?

- If not, which of the ethical types is most reflective of the way in which you resolved ethical or moral questions in the past?

- If your ethical type is reflective of your ethical decision making, is this ethical system desirable or worthy of continued use?

- Can you articulate the reasons why you hold such a preference?

- Can you articulate why your primary ethical type is superior to the others?

- Do any of the other ethical types have merit or value?

- Which ones?

- Why do these other ethical types appeal to you?

- What, if anything, is wrong with each of the other ethical types?

- Are there situations or circumstances where one of the other ethical types might be more preferable?

- How did you score in the other ethical types?

- To what extent do these other ethical types influence your decision making?

- Why are you influenced by them?

- Do any of the other ethical types have potential application for you?

- Why?

- Can you list the ethical types in the order in which they influence your ethical decision making?

- How do you deal with and resolve the competing influences of the different ethical types?

- Why did you score high in some and low in others?

- If none of the ethical types describe you, what, then, is the basis for your ethical decision making?

- How do your scores compare to the representative sample?

- Which, if any, scores significantly varied from the representative sample?

- Can you explain why there were variances?

- Can you explain why you scored the way you did?

- Which, if any, ethical type would you want your spouse, children, or other family members to rely on in their decision making?

- Why do you have this preference?

- What are your core ethical values?

- Can you list and articulate them to others?

- What ethical dilemmas now confront you?

- Can any of the ethical types help you make a better decision?

- Which ones? Why?

- Is there room for growth with respect to how you resolve ethical dilemmas?

- If so, what are the specific areas of growth?

- If not, why is there no room for growth?

- What, if anything, does this say about you?

- How have you resolved ethical and moral dilemmas in the past?

- Do you regret any ethical choices that you have made?

- If so, why?

- What can you learn from these past experiences in relation to your ethical type?

- How do you respond when someone disagrees with your ethical positions?

- What does this suggest about your ethical constitution?

- Are you tolerant of other ethical views?

- What does this attitude suggest about your ethics?

If you spend quality time in contemplation of these questions and the issues they raise, you will undoubtedly gain a much deeper appreciation of your ethical makeup. It is an exercise that is well worth the effort.

Understanding Others

Once you have achieved an understanding of your own ethical type, you can use the six ethical types to gain an understanding and appreciation of how others resolve, justify, and defend their ethical positions. If you study and remember the six ethical types, and if during an ethical discussion you listen carefully to what is being said, you will easily recognize the underlying ethical type that the other person relies on. This recognition and awareness of the influence of the underlying ethical type will give you a deeper understanding of the other person's ethical constitution. Additionally, your knowledge of the six ethical types should help you understand that human belief systems are as diverse as race, gender, age, and religion. Hopefully this will result in greater tolerance of opposing views.

You can increase your understanding of others by doing the following:

- Share your ethical type scores with others who have taken **The Ethical Type Indicator.**

- Ask others to share their ethical type scores with you.

- Ask your spouse, children, family, friends, and colleagues to characterize how they perceive your ethical type.

- Try to detect and characterize the ethical types of those you encounter.

- Share your ethical core values with others.

- Ask others to share their ethical core values with you.

- Ask others why they chose their specific ethical core values.

- Explain the six ethical types to others during an ethical discussion.

- Encourage others to take **The Ethical Type Indicator.**

USING THE ETHICAL TYPES

Communication Device

If you know the ethical type of another person, this awareness allows for a powerful and effective application of **The Ethical Type Indicator.** For example, if you are engaged in a discussion in which you are attempting to persuade a colleague to adopt a particular view on a matter, your chances of success are increased and enhanced if you know your colleague's primary ethical type and you develop and present arguments based on your colleague's ethical belief system.

Too often we attempt to persuade others to our point of view by bombarding them with facts, figures, analysis, and arguments that support our particular ethical belief system. We become frustrated when our logic fails to persuade others to adopt our views. This failure should be understandable when you recognize that a Utilitarian logic (if this is your primary ethical type) is incompatible with an Existential philosophy (if this is the other's primary ethical type). This is analogous to putting a round peg into a square hole. It is much easier to do when you adapt the circular peg to a square-like object of similar size. This is done by simply presenting arguments based on the other person's ethical type.

The results can be remarkable if you can properly detect the other person's ethical type and you are creative enough to develop arguments based on this type that will support your ethical view.

The key is to discover the other person's ethical type. This can be done by doing the following:

- Always ask the other person to explain the underlying rationale for an ethical position.

- Listen carefully to what is said and categorize the rationale into one of the six ethical types.

- Restate or paraphrase the other person's viewpoint using the language of the ethical type you believe the other is relying on.

- Ask for confirmation that you have correctly understood the other person's point of view.

- If you get confirmation, then creatively find facts, figures, analysis, and arguments based on that ethical type which support your position.

As you become more at ease with the technique, you will find it to be much more successful than a head-on attack based on your own ethical preference.

*Can you
identify, articulate, and
defend your core ethical values?*

CORE ETHICAL VALUES

Your moral and ethical decision making is influenced not only by your ethical type, but also by your core ethical values.

Core ethical values are those deeply held beliefs that you hold near and dear to your heart. They are those fundamental convictions that form the basis of your behavior and your view of the world.

These deeply held beliefs serve as beacons or guideposts in times of ethical or moral uncertainty and confusion. They are the anchors that, if remembered and followed, will keep you on your chosen moral path.

Core ethical values include concepts such as loyalty, truth, respect, friendship, work, family, honesty, kindness, trust, obedience, autonomy, bravery, courage, humility, etc. The list is endless.

Each of us has our own unique core ethical values. The challenge is to identify, understand, and follow them when confronted with ethical or moral dilemmas.

Can you identify and articulate your core ethical values? Do you know what principles guide your life?

The answers to the following questions will help you identify your core ethical values:

- Where do you spend your time?

- What do you spend your money on?

- What is truly important to you?

- How have you reacted to certain critical incidents in your life?

- Do your espoused values align with how you actually behave in your life?

- What will others say about you and your core ethical values?

Write the answers to the above questions and then spend time thinking about how your answers reflect your core ethical values.

Make a list of your core ethical values. List them in the order of importance to you.

Reflective judgment begins with understanding yourself and the way in which you resolve ethical dilemmas.

The process of ethical reasoning begins with understanding yourself and how you resolve ethical or moral dilemmas. *The Ethical Type Indicator* can be the catalyst and the foundation for this process of self-discovery. Once this inward journey is complete and you have a basis for understanding yourself and your ethical constitution, the challenge becomes one of choosing to either ratify your existing ethical makeup or change it to a more enlightened ethical belief system. This choice is entirely up to you. It is a highly personal experience that can be revealing and rewarding.

Once you have taken this step, you must learn a disciplined process of critical thinking or reflective judgment in order to wisely resolve ethical or moral dilemmas. This process of ethical reasoning requires emotional discipline, intellectual integrity, inner reflection, and the conscious exercise of free will.

Emotional discipline means the ability to recognize that ethical and moral issues stimulate highly emotional human responses that are often the result of unconscious conditioned reflexes. These reflexes contain prejudices, biases, stereotypes, and paradigms that have been handed down to us by our parents, family, churches, schools, peer groups, and business associations. Our own unique human experiences have further shaped and influenced these reflexes. Emotional discipline also refers to the ability to isolate these initial emotional responses so that your intellectual capacities can operate.

Intellectual integrity refers to the human capacity to engage in pure intellectual thought and honest analysis of the facts and issues involved in any ethical or moral controversy.

Inner reflection is the process of pausing, critically thinking about, and contemplating on the moral and ethical issues and implications presented by the dilemma.

The conscious exercise of free will means that you must make a deliberate choice as to how to resolve the dilemma. As humans, we have the ability to control our thoughts, emotions, and behavior. This autonomy is known as "free will." Ethical and moral dilemmas are best resolved by the conscious and deliberate exercise of free will.

When confronted with an ethical or a moral dilemma, the following 12 steps are recommended as an effective process to combine emotional discipline, intellectual integrity, inner reflection, and the conscious exercise of free will.

1. **Recognize the emotional reflex.**
   Recognize that emotional reflexes are operating to influence your decision. You must balance these strong emotions so that you can bring to bear your intellectual capacities to reason. This means that you must not jump to a conclusion, but consciously remind yourself to reserve final judgment until after you have given rational thought to the dilemma and your options.

2. **Identify the real ethical or moral issues.**
   Often, decisions are made without carefully considering the true underlying issue at hand. Thus, it is important that you identify, characterize, and articulate the specific issues presented by the dilemma.

3. **Gather relevant facts.**
   Don't assume that you have all the facts necessary to render a wise and ethical decision. Devote time to the process of confirming the existing facts and obtaining additional relevant information.

4. **Consider the law.**
   Determine if there are applicable legal requirements that affect the decision. If so, follow the law.

5. **Ask others for input.**
   Don't hesitate to seek input from others. Weigh the advice carefully. People see the world differently and have various perspectives. There is a natural tendency for people to influence and persuade you into adopting their notion of right and wrong.

6. **Consider your ethical belief system.**
   Remember that your ethical type is based on a specific philosophical belief system. If you have answered the questions on pages 18 through 20, you will have a firm grasp on your ethical type. Analyze and apply your belief system to the dilemma in relation to the facts that you have at your disposal.

7. **Consider your core ethical values.**
   Your core ethical values are guideposts that you should consider before making any final decision. Remember these values are those strongly held beliefs that you have chosen as beacons to guide you throughout your life. Make sure your decision reflects these values and is consistent with them.

8. **Consciously exercise your free will.**
   Remember that you have "free will," which is the ability to control your thoughts, emotions, and behavior. This uniquely human quality means that you have the freedom to choose your path. Make a conscious decision based on your belief system and core ethical values.

9. **Let the decision ripen.**
   Give yourself the opportunity to reconsider your decision in the light of a new day. Sleep on the decision before finalizing it.

10. Ratify or change the decision.
Once time has passed and you have had an opportunity to reconsider, either ratify or change the decision.

11. Announce the decision.
If possible, tell others about the decision. Going public has a tendency to hold you accountable to your decision.

12. Act on the decision.
Once you have announced the decision, implement it and adapt your behavior accordingly.

This process of ethical reasoning is not complicated. It just requires discipline. If you follow these steps and actually engage in this critical process of ethical reasoning, chances are you will make more enlightened ethical decisions.

A good way to exercise emotional discipline and engage your rational mind is to develop a set of questions that you ask yourself when confronted with an ethical decision.

Here are 20 questions that might be helpful when you encounter your next ethical dilemma:

1. Will my decision or conduct comply with the law?

2. Will my decision or conduct be consistent with my personal ethical belief system?

3. Will my decision or conduct reflect and promote my core ethical values?

4. What ethical principles or values ought to be the basis of my decision or conduct in this situation?

5. Have I considered the needs and interests of those who might be affected by my decision or conduct?

6. Will my decision be judged fair now and in the future?

7. Will I be proud of my decision?

8. What will my family think of me if they know or learn of my behavior?

9. Will my decision or conduct create value?

10. Will my decision or conduct move me closer to goodness and virtue?

11. Am I being pressured or unduly influenced by others?

12. Am I being driven by my emotions?

13. Have I filtered out my ego needs and my own self-interests?

14. Will my conduct reflect honesty, integrity, and truthfulness?

15. Are there spiritual insights or principles I ought to consider?

16. What will be the consequences of my behavior?

17. Who will benefit from my decision or conduct?

18. Who will be harmed by my conduct?

19. Will my decision or conduct permit or encourage exploitation of others or greed?

20. Are there other alternatives I should consider?

*People tend to react emotionally
to an ethical dilemma and
often fail to utilize the power of
the rational, contemplative mind.*

*The process of reflective judgment
requires emotional discipline,
intellectual integrity, inner reflection,
and the conscious exercise of free will
toward a noble or just end.*

*Does your personal conduct
align with your
stated ethical beliefs?*

If you want to know
a person's beliefs, listen not
to what he or she may say,
but look closely at what
he or she does and how
they live their life.

OTHER RESOURCES

HRD Press also offers the following resources for those interested in using the *Ethical Type Indicator* as a training tool and learning more about ethics:

- *The Ethical Type Indicator Instructor's Manual.*

- *Ethical Virtuosity: Seven Steps to Help You Discover and Do the Right Thing At the Right Time*

Louie Larimer, author of the *Ethical Type Indicator,* is available for in-house training at your organization. Contact him at 719-636-8983.